RELIGION

LIFE IN THE ROMAN EMPIRE
RELIGION

BY

KATHRYN HINDS

BENCHMARK BOOKS

MARSHALL CAVENDISH
NEW YORK

Alenae, discipula studiosa linguae latinae

The author and publisher wish to specially thank J. Brett McClain
of the Oriental Institute of the University of Chicago
for his invaluable help in reading the manuscript.

⌖

Benchmark Books Marshall Cavendish   99 White Plains Road   Tarrytown, New York 10591-9001
www.marshallcavendish.com   Copyright © 2005 by Marshall Cavendish Corporation   All rights
reserved. No part of this book may be reproduced or utilized in any form or by any means electronic
or mechanical including photocopying, recording, or by any information storage and retrieval system, without permission from the copyright holders.   All Internet sites were available and accurate
when this book was sent to press.   Book design by Michael Nelson   LIBRARY OF CONGRESS
CATALOGING-IN-PUBLICATION DATA: Hinds, Kathryn, 1962- Religion / by Kathryn Hinds.   p. cm.
— (Life in the Roman empire)   Includes bibliographical references and index.   ISBN 0-7614-1657-9
1. Rome—Religion. I. Title II. Series: Hinds, Kathryn, 1962- . Life in the Roman empire.
BL803.H56 2004   292'.07—dc22   2004008400

Art Research: Rose Corbett Gordon, Mystic CT
Front cover: The Art Archive/Archaeological Museum, Naples/Dagli Orti Back cover: Louvre Museum,
Paris/Lauros/Giraudon/Bridgeman Art Library Pages i, 1, 10, 13, 18, 24: The Art Archive/Archaeological
Museum, Naples/Dagli Orti; page iii: Alinari/Art Resource, NY; page vi: Index/Bridgeman Art Library;
page viii: Fitzwilliam Museum, University of Cambridge, UK/Bridgeman Art Library; page 3: Ashmolean
Museum, University of Oxford, UK/Bridgeman Art Library; page 4: The Art Archive/Museo Nazionale
Terme, Rome/Dagli Orti; page 5: Lincolnshire County Council, Usher Gallery, Lincoln, UK/Bridgeman
Art Library; page 6: Arasta Mosaic Museum, Istanbul/Bridgeman Art Library; page 8: Ancient Art and
Architecture Collection Ltd./Bridgeman Art Library; page 9: The Art Archive/Muzeul de Constantza,
Romania/Dagli Orti; page 12: Louvre Museum, Paris/Lauros/ Giraudon/Bridgeman Art Library; pages
15, 74: The Art Archive/Museo Opitergino Oderzo, Treviso/Dagli Orti; page 17: The Art Archive/Museo
Prenestino Palestrina/Dagli Orti; page 20: Phillips, The International Fine Art Auctioneers, UK/Bridge-
man Art Library; page 22: Origlia France/Corbis Sygma; page 25: Charles Plante Fine Arts/Bridgeman
Art Library;   page 26: Lauros/Giraudon/Bridgeman Art Library;   page 28: Hadrian's Villa, Tivoli,
Italy/Bridgeman Art Library; page 30: Scala/Art Resource, NY; page 33: Werner Forman/Art Resource,
NY; pages 34, 38, 68: Araldo de Luca/Corbis; pages 36, 37, 44, 58, The Art Archive/Musée du Louvre,
Paris/Dagli Orti; page 39: The Art Archive/Archaeological Museum, Ostia/Dagli Orti; pages 40, 46: Villa
dei Misteri, Pompeii/Bridgeman Art Library; page 43: The Art Archive/Museo della Civilta Romana,
Rome/Dagli Orti; page 45: Louvre, Paris/Bridgeman Art Library; pages 47, 50: Erich Lessing/Art
Resource, NY; page 51: Mimmo Jodice/Corbis; page 52 top: The British Museum/HIP/Topham/The
Image Works; page 52 bottom: Museo e Gallerie Nazionali di Capodimonte, Naples/Bridgeman Art
Library; page 53: The Art Archive/Museo Civico, Trieste/Dagli Orti; page 55: The Art Archive/Dagli Orti;
page 56: The Forbes Magazine Collection, New York/Bridgeman Art Library; page 60: Christie's Images,
London, UK/Bridgeman Art Library; page 61: Galleria degli Uffizi, Florence/Bridgeman Art Library;
page 63: The Art Archive/Galleria d'Arte Moderna, Rome/Dagli Orti; page 66: Musée Crozatier, Le Puy-en-
Velay, France/, Giraudon/Bridgeman Art Library; page 67: The Art Archive; page 71: Bargello, Flo-
rence/Bridgeman Art Library; page 72: Louvre, Paris/Peter Willi/Bridgeman Art Library

Printed in China
1 3 5 6 4 2

front cover: A fresco of Victoria, the goddess of victory, from Pompeii
back cover: This second-century marble relief shows some of the preparations for a sacrifice.
half-title page: The god Bacchus and one of his female followers
title page: A bull is led to a temple for sacrifice as part of a religious celebration.
About the Roman Empire, p. vi: Diana, goddess of hunting, prepares to draw her bow.

CONTENTS

ABOUT THE ROMAN EMPIRE

When we think about the Roman Empire, we often picture gladiators, chariot races, togas, marble statues, and legions on the march. These images tell only part of the story of ancient Rome. According to the Romans themselves, their city was founded in 753 B.C.E.* At first Rome was ruled by kings, then it became a republic. In 27 B.C.E. Augustus Caesar became Rome's absolute ruler—its first emperor. Meanwhile, this city built on seven hills overlooking the Tiber River had been steadily expanding its power. In Augustus's time Rome controlled all of Italy and the rest of mainland Europe west of the Rhine River and south of the Danube River, as well as much of North Africa and the Middle East.

At its height, the Roman Empire reached all the way from Britain to Persia. It brought together an array of European, African, and Middle Eastern peoples, forming a vibrant multicultural society. During much of the empire's existence, its various ethnic and religious groups got along with remarkable tolerance and understanding—a model that can still inspire us today. We can also be inspired by the Romans' tremendous achievements in the arts, architecture, literature, law, and philosophy, just as they have inspired and influenced people in Europe and the Americas for hundreds of years.

So step back in time, and visit Rome at its most powerful, from 27 B.C.E. to around 200 C.E., the first two centuries of the empire. In this book you will meet priests and priestesses, emperors and poets, and worshippers at various stages of their lives. These people had many of the same joys and sorrows, hopes and fears that we do, but their world was very different from ours. Forget about telephones, computers, cars, and televisions, and imagine what it might have been like to live among the people who ruled much of the ancient world. Welcome to life in the Roman Empire. . . .

* A variety of systems of dating have been used by different cultures throughout history. Many historians now prefer to use B.C.E (Before Common Era) and C.E. (Common Era) instead of B.C. (Before Christ) and A.D. (Anno Domini), out of respect for the diversity of the world's peoples. In this book, all dates are C.E. unless otherwise noted.

· I ·

A WORLD OF GODS AND SPIRITS

ROME IS A PLACE WORTHY OF THE PRESENCE OF ALL THE GODS.
—OVID, *FASTI*

he Roman Empire was a melting pot of religious attitudes and beliefs. Some people were passionately devoted to the gods; others probably went through the forms of religious ceremonies mainly for the sake of tradition. Many others stood between these two positions. People in the provinces often continued to worship as they had before their lands were conquered by Rome, but Roman religion also came to the provinces. Similarly, religious traditions from outside Italy made their way to Rome and became part of the Romans' belief system.

Religion was extremely important to the Roman state and to the Romans' sense of themselves. As the great orator and statesman Cicero wrote shortly before Augustus came to power, "If we com-

opposite:
Jupiter was the chief god of the Roman state and its special protector.

1

pare our history to that of other nations, we shall see that although we may be equal or inferior to them in other respects, we outshine them by far in religion, that is to say, in the worship of the gods." A centerpiece of Roman belief was the concept of *pax deorum,* "the peace of the gods"—the state of harmony and order that came with the proper relationship between humans and the deities. As long as the Roman people did their part to maintain *pax deorum,* it was believed, they and their empire would thrive. Gods and humans, after all, were members of the same community.

DIVINE POWERS

The Romans, like many peoples, felt that there was a kind of divine force or spirit present in every activity, in everything in the natural world, and even in the objects of daily life. This spirit was often called a *numen* (the plural form is *numina*). Awareness of the *numina* gave pious Romans the sense that the divine took part in all they did, wherever they went. For example, when they entered or left their homes, they were interacting with the *numen* of the threshold, Limentinus; when they swept the floor, the *numen* Deverra was present in the broom. A farmer tending his grain crop saw the powers of many *numina* at work, including Seia, the guardian of the seed while it was underground; Segetia, the spirit of the ripening grain aboveground; and Messor, the *numen* of harvesting.

Abstract ideas, too, had their *numina*. These were often personified as deities, usually goddesses, such as Fortuna (Luck), Pax (Peace), and Victoria (Victory). Similarly, the *numina* of provinces and cities were portrayed and honored as goddesses: for example, Britannia (Britain) and Roma (Rome). River spirits might be thought of as male or female: the Tiber River in Italy was watched over by the god Tiberinus, while the goddess Sequana was the personification of the Seine River in what is now France. As these examples show, there might not be a clear-cut difference between *numina* and deities. In general, we can say that all deities were *numina*—divine powers—but many *numina* were not imagined to take on human characteristics as gods or goddesses.

GUARDIANS OF HOME AND FAMILY

Every individual also had a *numen* or guardian spirit. This was known as a *genius* for a man and a *iuno* for a woman. The Genius Paterfamilias was the spirit of the father of the family, the head of the household. It was often symbolized as a snake. This *genius* protected not only the father, but also everyone else in the household, for whom the father was responsible.

Associated with the Genius Paterfamilias was the Lar, another kind of household guardian. Every family had its own particular Lar; some scholars think that the Lares (LAH-rays) were related to spirits of the family's ancestors. In artwork, Lares were often portrayed as dancing young men. They were so closely linked to the home that a Roman expression for "returning home" was *redire ad Larem suum:* "to go back to one's Lar." Along with the Lares, Roman families honored their household's Penates (pe-NAH-tays), guardians of the pantry or food cupboard. There were also public Penates, whose worship was related to the well-being of Rome, as well as Lares who were honored at crossroads in every district of the city.

This bronze statuette of a Lar stood in an honored place in a Roman home.

The hearth fire of each home was under the guardianship of the goddess Vesta, who was generally worshipped alongside the family Lares and Penates. Proper worship of Vesta was considered essential to the well-being of Rome. In her temple in the Forum, the heart of the city, the goddess was symbolized by an eternal flame, which was tended by a group of priestesses called the Vestal Virgins.

THE GREAT GODS

While the Lares, Penates, and many *numina* had very specific areas of concern, the major deities looked after a wide range of interests. They were also felt to be particularly involved with the well-being of Rome and its empire. For this reason, they are often called the gods of the state religion. This was the official, formal religion of the empire and was full of time-honored traditions that maintained the relationship between the Romans and their gods.

Juno, the goddess who watched over women, childbirth, and marriage

Chief among the deities was Jupiter, known as the Best and Greatest. He was the chief protector of Rome, the giver of victory, and the guardian of emperors. In addition, like his Greek counterpart, Zeus, he was a god of the sky and the weather, especially thunderstorms. He also watched over agreements, contracts, and promises. Jupiter was often symbolized by an eagle.

Juno was the wife of Jupiter. She was particularly connected with women and marriage, but had other concerns as well. Like many Roman deities, she had a number of titles, which came from the various roles she played. Often she was called Juno Regina, "Juno the Queen." As Juno Lucina she was a goddess of light and of childbirth. She also had a military aspect and could be approached as Juno Curitis, "Juno of the Spear." Juno Sospita meant "Juno the Savior," referring to her role as a protector. Juno was closely identified with the Greek goddess Hera.

Minerva was mainly a goddess of crafts and warfare. As Minerva Medica, she was concerned with doctors and healing. In art she was generally shown wearing a helmet and might be holding a spear and shield, as was the corresponding Greek goddess, Athena.

Mars, often equated with the Greek Ares, is most familiar to us today as the Roman god of war. In the ancient world, however, he was also a protector of the crops and a god of springtime, when seeds were planted—this is why the month of March was named after him. Wolves and woodpeckers were sacred to Mars.

Venus, too, played various roles. We know her best as the goddess of love and beauty, like her Greek counterpart, Aphrodite. But Venus was also the *numen* of gardens, making them fertile to produce vegetables, fruit, and flowers. The Romans honored her as their divine ancestress, for she was the mother of Aeneas. This legendary hero, a refugee from the Trojan War, settled in Italy near the future site of Rome, and his descendant, Romulus, was said to have founded the city.

Mercurius, or Mercury, was the messenger of the gods. He was also a deity of abundance, trade, and success in business. Artists often portrayed Mercury in the same way as the Greek god Hermes, wearing winged shoes and a winged hat, carrying a staff with two snakes entwined around it (called a caduceus).

Other major Roman deities included Ceres, goddess of grain

Mercurius rests from a journey, his staff lying at his feet. An eighteenth-century English sculptor created this marble statue in the Roman style.

(equivalent to Greece's Demeter); Diana (Artemis), goddess of women, wild nature, hunting, and the moon; Apollo (whose name was the same in Greek), god of healing, prophecy, poetry, music, and the sun; Neptune (Poseidon), god of the sea and of horses; Hercules (Heracles), god of victory, strength, and business deals; Volcanus or Vulcan (Hephaestus to the Greeks), god of fire and metalworking; Pomona, goddess of fruit; Vertumnus, god of orchards and the changing seasons; Silvanus, a god of woodlands; and Castor, a god of horses, horsemen, athletes, and sailors. As can be seen,

A mosaic of the sea god Neptune surrounded by fish

most of the deities of the state religion were felt to be quite similar to gods and goddesses from Greece. In fact, people in the eastern part of the empire usually worshipped the deities under their Greek names.

DIVINE HONORS FOR THE EMPEROR

Many peoples of the ancient Mediterranean world, including the Romans, did not draw a sharp line between the human and the divine. They recognized certain qualities as being godlike, and it was fairly easy to believe that people with those qualities could in fact become gods. The abilities to command armies, to win victories, to make laws, to govern peoples—these were all seen as having a kind of divine nature. It is not surprising, then, that the emperors, who wielded such powers, received divine honors.

The emperor Augustus was the adopted son of Julius Caesar, who was regarded as a god after his death. This made Augustus the son of a god, which increased his own authority. In some eastern provinces of the empire, where rulers had always been considered at least semidivine, Augustus and his successors were honored as gods not only after their deaths, but during their lifetimes as well. In Rome itself, however, Augustus refused to be worshipped. Instead, he encouraged people to honor his *genius*. Worshipping the emperor's guardian spirit quickly became an established and expected part of the state religion.

After Augustus died, he, like Julius Caesar, was officially deified (made a god)—as with Caesar, his achievements seemed superhuman. This was not the case with some of the succeeding emperors. In fact, the empire's third and fifth rulers, Gaius Caligula and Nero, were both egomaniacs who sought to be worshipped in Rome as gods during their lifetimes—for this and other reasons, both were hated by much of the Roman populace. The fourth emperor, Claudius, did better. He was deified after his death, for he had conquered Britain (something that even Caesar had not managed to do). By the last quarter of the first century, it was expected that all but the worst emperors would join the ranks of the gods after death. And so as the emperor Vespasian lay dying in 79 C.E., he was able to joke, "Alas, I suppose I am becoming a god."

PERSONAL SAVIORS

In addition to worshipping the great gods who ensured the well-being of the Roman people as a whole, individuals were often drawn to goddesses and gods who offered a more personal relationship. Many people were devoted to Aesculapius (in Greek, Asklepios), a god of healing. Worshippers in poor health might spend a night, or several nights, in his temple in the hope of receiving healing dreams from the god. These dreams could bring

comfort, if nothing else. The orator and teacher Aelius Aristides had such an experience in a temple of Aesculapius in 146. He described "a feeling as of taking hold of him [the god] and of clearly perceiving that he himself had come, . . . and of hearing some things as in a dream, some waking; hair stood straight, tears flowed in joy; the burden of understanding seemed light."

The background of this relief shows a young man, assisted by a priest, going to sleep in the temple of Aesculapius. In the foreground, the god comes to the young man in a dream and heals his injured arm.

Throughout the empire, the Egyptian goddess Isis inspired intense devotion. Many of her worshippers believed that all other goddesses were Isis under different names, playing different roles. Even under her own name, she was concerned with a great many things, among them love, childbirth, motherhood, healing, agriculture, weather, navigation, language, law, justice, war, and peace. Isis was a compassionate, merciful goddess who cared about the lives of those who prayed to her. Moreover, she could overrule the decrees of fate. She had restored her murdered husband, Osiris, to life, and so she also assured her followers a blessed afterlife.

Another deity who promised life after death was the god Bacchus. On one level, he was simply the god of wine, but in addition he represented freedom and ecstasy. He was identified with grapevines, which died back in winter and then came to life again in the spring. Cybele, or Magna Mater (meaning "The Great Mother"); Mithras, a god of light and truth; and the Greek earth goddesses Demeter and Persephone were also major deities who offered eternal life and the salvation or care of an individual's soul.

ᵔᵃ ISIS, THE MOTHER OF ALL ᵉˢ

The Golden Ass, a novel by the second-century author Apuleius, tells the story of a man named Lucius who meddles in magic that he doesn't understand. As a result, he is turned into a donkey, and in this shape he has many adventures and endures great suffering. At last, on the verge of despair, he sees the full moon rising over the sea and is inspired to pray for help. The goddess Isis appears to him in a dream and tells him how he can regain his human form. After he is restored to himself, he devotes the rest of his life to serving the goddess. Here is one of his prayers in praise of her, which expresses feelings shared by real-life worshippers of Isis:

Most holy and everlasting Redeemer of the human race, you munificently cherish our lives and bestow the consoling smiles of a Mother upon our tribulations. There is no day or night, not so much as the minutest fraction of time, that is not stuffed with the eternity of your mercy. You protect men on land and sea. You chase the storms of life and stretch out the hand of succour to the dejected. You can untwine the hopelessly tangled threads of the Fates. You can mitigate the tempests of Fortune and check the stars in the courses of their malice. The gods of heaven worship you. The gods of hell bow before you. You rotate the globe. You light the sun. You govern space. You trample hell. The stars move to your orders, the seasons return, the gods rejoice, the elements combine. At your nod the breezes blow, clouds collect, seeds sprout, blossoms increase. The birds that fly in the air, the beasts that roam on the hills, the serpents that hide in the earth, the monsters that swim in the ocean, tremble before your majesty.

II

BELIEFS AND CEREMONIES

AND WHAT REASON HAVE THE GODS FOR DOING DEEDS
OF KINDNESS? IT IS THEIR NATURE.
—SENECA, *MORAL LETTERS*

he Roman state religion was practical, concerned with the here and now—the health, prosperity, and security of family, community, and empire. Religion and daily life were intertwined, and both were guided by the concept of *pietas*. The Romans understood this word to mean a proper sense of duty that encompassed all areas of life. *Pietas* involved conscientiously upholding correct, respectful relations with parents and other family members, ancestors, fellow citizens, government authorities—and deities. A person with *pietas* was careful to honor the gods by performing the traditional prayers and ceremonies of the state religion. These had clearly pleased the gods in the past, as the empire's strength proved, and so the established observances would continue to win divine favor for the Romans.

opposite:
An important part of many Roman religious rites was the offering of animals, such as this bull, in sacrifice to the gods.

OFFERINGS AND PRAYERS

The central part of most Roman religious rites was sacrifice. This was, literally, a sacred action, which involved making an offering to the gods. Because the deities gave so much to humans, it was considered only proper to give something back to them. The offerings could be fruit, flowers, wheat cakes or crackers, milk, wine, honey, or burning incense. They were often made on an altar before a statue of a goddess or god.

Major ceremonies generally called for "blood sacrifice," which would take place at an outdoor altar. Although this practice may be difficult to understand today, it was common in ancient times. In the Roman Empire, an animal would be chosen depending on the ceremony's purpose and the deity being honored. For example, a cow would be sacrificed to Juno, but a bull to Mars. The animal had to be perfect in health and appearance, and it could not struggle as it was led to the altar—an obviously unwilling victim was unac-

A sacrificial bull is held by two *victimarii*, the priestly assistants who will kill him as quickly and humanely as possible, while a flute player provides music for the ceremony.

ceptable to the gods. At the altar, a priest* burned incense and made a libation, or liquid offering, of wine. Then he consecrated the animal by sprinkling it with ground and salted grain (called *mola salsa*), pouring wine onto its head, and passing a knife over its back. An assistant then killed the animal; this was done swiftly, with as little pain as possible.

Sometimes the whole body was dedicated to the deity and burned on the altar, but usually only certain parts were burned. The rest of the animal either provided meat for a feast among the priests and worshippers or was taken to be sold in the marketplace. Describing the feasting after a sacrifice, the author and philosopher Plutarch wrote, "It's not the abundance of wine or the roasting of meat that makes the joy of sharing a table in a temple, but the good hope and belief that the god is present in his kindness and graciously accepts what is offered."

A Pompeian couple making preparations for a sacrifice. The woman is setting out a *patera*, a shallow bowl used for pouring libations.

Sacrifices were always accompanied by prayers. These had to take a specific form, as the scholar Pliny the Elder explained:

It apparently does no good to offer a sacrifice or to consult the gods with due ceremony unless you also speak words of prayer. In addition, some words are appropriate for seeking favorable omens, others for warding off evil, and still others for securing help. We notice, for example, that our highest

*In many circumstances, government officials, army commanders, and fathers of families could also function as priests and preside over sacrifices.

magistrates make appeals to the gods with specific and set prayers. And in order that no word be omitted or spoken out of turn, one attendant reads the prayer from a book, another is assigned to check it closely, a third is appointed to enforce silence. In addition, a flutist plays to block out any extraneous [distracting] sounds.

Roman prayers were very carefully worded. For example, if a farmer had to clear a woodland, he would want to make a sacrifice to the deity who watched over it—but he might not know for certain who that deity was. So his prayer would be phrased along these lines: "Whether you are a god or a goddess to whom this grove is sacred, as it is proper to sacrifice to you a pig as an offering to make up for disturbing this sacred place, whether I or someone I have appointed performs the sacrifice, I pray that you will show goodwill to me, my home, and my family." Prayers could also take the form of vows, in which the worshipper asked the deity to do something and promised to do something in return—usually to perform a sacrifice or set up an altar or statue to the goddess or god in question. Poorer people might give a small plaque or clay figurine to a temple in fulfillment of a vow.

In another kind of prayer (which scholars sometimes call a curse or hex), a person called on a deity to take action against a thief or other enemy. These prayers were often inscribed on sheets of lead and left in the temple of the god who was being appealed to. One example from southern Britain reads, "A memorandum to the god Mercury . . . from Saturnina a woman concerning the linen cloth she has lost. Let him who stole it not have rest before/unless/until he brings the aforesaid things to the temple, whether he is man or woman, slave or free."

⁓ EVERYDAY MAGIC ⬧

Almost everyone in the Roman world believed in magic. Most people didn't have much problem with it, so long as it was not used to harm others. And sometimes what seems like magic or superstition was probably, to those involved, simply a way of praying or of being mindful of the role of the gods in their everyday lives. Or a "superstitious" practice might have been just a traditional custom whose religious meaning had long been forgotten. This passage from Pliny the Elder's *Natural History* shows how much religion, magic, and customary behaviors could overlap:

There is indeed nobody who does not fear to be spell-bound by imprecations [curses]. . . . On walls too are written prayers to avert fires. . . . The dictator Caesar, after one serious accident to his carriage, is said always, as soon as he was seated, to have been in the habit of repeating three times a formula or prayer for a safe journey, a thing we know that most people do today.

. . . Why on the first day of the year do we wish one another cheerfully a happy and prosperous New Year? . . . Why on mentioning the dead do we protest that their memory is not being attacked by us? Why do we believe that in all matters the odd numbers are more powerful. . . ? Why at the harvest of the fruits do we say: "These are old," and pray for the new ones to take their place? Why do we say "Good health" to those who sneeze? . . . Moreover, according to an accepted belief absent people can divine [know] by the ringing in their ears that they are the object of talk. . . .

We certainly have formulas to charm away hail, various diseases, and burns, some actually tested by experience, but I am very shy of quoting them, because of the widely different feelings they arouse. Wherefore everyone must form his own opinion about them as he pleases.

LEARNING THE WILL OF THE GODS

When Romans made a blood sacrifice, they generally wanted some sign that the deity had accepted the sacrifice and looked favorably on the worshipper. For this reason, men known as *haruspices* were called on to examine the animal's internal organs. A *haruspex* knew the normal shape, color, and condition of the organs. If there were deformities or other differences from what was normal, the *haruspex* understood what these symbolized. The Romans believed that the gods "imprinted" the marks of their favor or disfavor on the organs as the animal was being consecrated. If the signs showed that the sacrifice was unacceptable, a further sacrifice would have to be made.

Before a person took any major action, it was important to find out if the gods approved. This was another occasion when a *haruspex* might be called on to examine the organs of a sacrificed animal. In this case, if the signs were unfavorable, the person could abandon the project, wait until the signs were better, find some way to earn the gods' favor—or go ahead as planned and risk divine displeasure. But most Romans knew plenty of stories about what could happen to people who took these risks, such as generals who ignored the gods' warnings and suffered dreadful defeats.

Another way of learning whether the gods approved of an action or not was augury. This was also known as "taking the auspices." Augury generally involved marking out a particular area, in the sky or on the ground, and then watching and interpreting the behavior of birds in that area, especially eagles, vultures, and crows or ravens. The priests who explained what the birds' flight patterns and eating habits meant were called augurs. They were

Worshippers
in Roman-ruled
Egypt hold
a riverside
ceremony to
seek the goodwill
of the gods of
the Nile.

also responsible for marking out various kinds of sacred boundaries, such as the places where temples would be built.

The deities could send warnings without being asked for them—sometimes through bolts of lightning, at other times through "prodigies." In general, prodigies were unusual happenings in the natural world, or they involved something being very out of place, such as a wild animal showing up within a city. *Haruspices* explained the meaning of lightning flashes and prodigies and recommended the proper actions to take in order to prevent the harm that was warned against. For example, when a horned owl—considered a very unlucky bird—was found in a temple in Rome in 43 C.E., the whole city had to be purified and protected with sacrifices, prayers, and a solemn procession around the *pomerium,* or sacred boundary line.

INITIATIONS

For a great many Romans, this world was the only one with which they concerned themselves. They either did not believe in an afterlife or did not worry themselves about it. Residents of the empire

This fresco from Herculaneum, Italy, shows initiates of the Mysteries of Isis taking part in a ceremony in honor of their goddess.

who were drawn to the worship of deities such as Isis and Bacchus, on the other hand, were a good deal more interested in the world beyond this one. These worshippers did not reject the state religion, but alongside it they wanted a spiritual path that had a greater mystical, emotional, and personal feeling.

These "in-depth" spiritual practices have come to be known as the Mysteries, or mystery religions. The term comes from Greek *mystes,* "an initiate." Initiates were people who went through a ceremony that brought them closer to a particular goddess or god, deepened their understanding of the spiritual dimension of life, and gave them a promise of overcoming death. The ceremonies were kept secret from outsiders, and in any case were difficult to describe in words. These experiences were highly symbolic, and only someone who had been through them would really understand the meaning of them. In general, however, we can tell that initiations usually included purification, spiritual ordeals or trials, beholding sacred symbols, hearing sacred chants or stories about the deity, and a symbolic death and rebirth. This is how the second-century orator and novelist Apuleius described initiation into the Mysteries of Isis:

> I approached the confines of death. I trod the threshold of Proserpine [the goddess of the Underworld]; and borne through the elements I returned. At midnight I saw the Sun shining in all his glory. I approached the gods below and the gods above, and I stood beside them, and I worshipped them. Behold, I have told my experience, and yet what you hear can mean nothing to you.

·III·

SACRED
PLACES

WE HAVE A CITY FOUNDED BY THE AUSPICES AND AUGURY;
THERE IS NOT A CORNER OF IT THAT IS NOT FULL OF . . . OUR GODS.
—LIVY, *AB URBE CONDITA*

laces were important in Roman religion. Rome itself was in many ways considered a sacred site, chosen by deities and heroes long ago as a place of greatness. One sign of the city's religious character was the *pomerium* that enclosed it. This boundary was a strip of land that set off the city as a sacred place. It was marked at every change of direction by six-foot-tall blocks of stone. Any emperor who enlarged the empire was allowed to also enlarge the *pomerium,* and this was done on several occasions. When the Romans founded a colony,* its *pomerium* was laid out just like Rome's. After the auspices were taken, the founder of the colony ceremonially plowed a furrow around the location. This procedure showed that colonies were intended to be "little Romes" where, among other things, the

opposite:
Many of Rome's sacred places no longer exist or are in ruins. Some, like this temple (shown in a twentieth-century painting), survived because they were later turned into Christian churches.

---

*A Roman colony was a settlement in Italy or the provinces for retiring soldiers and other citizens.

Roman deities would be honored. Whether in the capital or the colonies, burials were not allowed within the *pomerium,* for they would contaminate the holy ground.

HOUSES OF THE GODS

In his great epic *The Aeneid,* the poet Virgil included an episode in which the hero, Aeneas, is shown important landmarks of what will someday be the city of Rome. Among the sights is a hill covered with tangled thickets. Despite its wild and uninviting aspect, Aeneas is aware of the "god-haunted feel of the place." His guide tells him,

> In this grove, on this hill with leafy summit, there lives
> A god—but which god, we can't be certain. Yet some believe
> They've seen Jupiter himself, have often seen him brandish
> In his hand his dark shield when he stirs up the clouds.

The gods of Rome's Capitol, with their sacred birds sitting beside their right feet: an owl for Minerva (*far left*), an eagle for Jupiter (unfortunately, everything but its talons and part of a wing have broken off), and a peacock for Juno

After Rome was founded, this hill became the location of the Capitol, the great temple of Jupiter, Juno, and Minerva, together known as the Capitoline Triad. Many cities throughout the empire also came to have Capitols, dedicated to the same three deities. A Capitol was nearly always built on a hill or rise, generally close to the city's forum, or political center.

Inside the Capitol were statues of each member of the Triad. Each statue stood in its own *cella,* or room. Most temples, however, were dedicated to only one deity and so had only one *cella.* Classical Roman temples were rectangular in shape and elevated on a high platform called a podium, which might have storage areas beneath it. At the front of the temple a wide stairway led from the ground to the top of the podium. Here there was a columned porch, sometimes taking up as much as half the temple's length. The *cella,* enclosed by solid walls at the back and sides, was behind the porch.

The architect Vitruvius, writing during the reign of Augustus, recommended that, whenever possible, temples and statues face west:

> This will enable those who approach the altar with offerings or sacrifices to face the direction of the sunrise in facing the statue in the temple, and thus those who are undertaking vows look toward the quarter from which the sun comes forth, and likewise the statues themselves appear to be coming forth out of the east to look upon them as they pray and sacrifice.

A few Roman temples were circular. The temple of Vesta was built in this shape because it was intended to resemble the round huts in which the earliest Romans lived. Hercules also had a small, circular temple in Rome. A much grander building, though, was the

⌁ CEREMONIES FOR REBUILDING ⌁ A TEMPLE

In 69 C.E. Rome's Capitol was destroyed in a fire. The next year, the emperor Vespasian had this important temple rebuilt. The historian Tacitus described the ceremonies that began the reconstruction:

On June 21, beneath a cloudless sky, the entire space devoted to the sacred precinct was encircled with fillets [ribbons] and garlands. Soldiers who had auspicious names entered with boughs of good-omened trees. Next, the Vestal Virgins, together with boys and girls both of whose parents were alive, sprinkled it with water drawn from springs and rivers. Then the praetor [city official] Helvidius Priscus, in terms dictated by the pontiff [priest] Plautius Aelianus, having first purified the area with pig-sheep-bull sacrifices and placed the entrails on an altar of turf, prayed to Jupiter, Juno, and Minerva, and to the tutelary gods of the Empire, to prosper the undertaking and by their divine help to raise up their abodes begun by human piety. He then touched the fillets which were wound around the foundation stone and entwined around the ropes. At the same time the other magistrates, the priest, senators, *equites,* and a great part of the people, uniting their efforts with zeal and joy, dragged the huge stone. Everywhere there were thrown into the foundations contributions of silver and gold, and of virgin metals never smelted in furnaces but in their natural state; the soothsayers had previously declared that the work should not be defiled by stone or gold intended for any other purpose. The height of the temple was increased; this was the only variation which religious scruple permitted, and the one feature which had been thought wanting in the magnificence of the old temple.

The inside of a round Roman temple that has been converted into a church, drawn by an Italian artist around 1800

Pantheon, a temple like no other. Behind its porch was a huge rotunda, roofed with a spectacular dome. In the center of the dome was a wide circular opening to let in sunlight. The lofty dome was probably intended to represent the sky, with the opening symbolizing the sun. The deities worshipped in the Pantheon may have been those after whom the planets were named—we know that Venus and Mars, at least, were honored there.

ALTARS

Temples of the Roman state religion were not meant to hold groups of worshippers. An individual could go into a temple to honor the deity privately, burning incense or leaving an offering on a small altar before the statue of the goddess or god. Public, group worship took place outside the temple, focusing on an altar erected at the foot of the stairs. This was where all blood sacrifices performed at the temple took place. (Blood sacrifices had to be conducted outdoors, under the open sky.) Only the priest spoke during the ceremony; everyone else participated with their minds and hearts, but not with their voices.

All temples had altars, but altars did not need to be at temples.

Families had small altars in their homes and, quite often, outdoor altars on their property for blood sacrifices. Travelers sometimes set up roadside altars to thank a deity for protection on a journey. Some altars were part of open-air shrines, such as those dedicated to the Lares at crossroads in Rome. Small public altars were used for incense and other bloodless offerings.

Two very important altars—used for blood sacrifices—were the Ara Pacis, the "Altar of Peace," and the Ara Maxima, the "Greatest Altar." Both were located in Rome. The Ara Pacis was an impressive monument, dedicated by the emperor Augustus in 9 B.C.E. Made of marble, it was U-shaped and surrounded with a nearly square wall, twenty-three feet high, that had openings on the east and west sides. A low podium supported this whole complex. Both altar and wall were adorned with wonderful sculptured reliefs that included images

The Ara Pacis has been reconstructed near its original site. This is the front entrance; the stairs lead up to the actual altar. On the upper right of the wall, the hero Aeneas is shown preparing to make a sacrifice.

of Mother Earth, the emperor and his family, an episode from the story of Aeneas, and other legendary and ceremonial scenes.

The Ara Maxima was probably called the "Greatest" because of its ancientness. It was dedicated to Hercules, who was said to have set it up himself, making the first sacrifice at it. This altar was a place where businessmen often met to agree on deals, and where merchants sometimes came to pledge a tenth of their profits to Hercules. Women were not allowed to approach the Ara Maxima because, according to one legend, a priestess of Bona Dea ("The Good Goddess") once refused to give Hercules a drink of water from the goddess's sacred spring.

THE DIVINE IN NATURE

Many places and objects in the natural world had a religious significance. Sources of rivers, hot springs, groves of trees, and the like were felt to be holy places, where divine powers were strongly present. Worshippers might set up shrines or altars to deities on these sites, or there could even be full-blown temples. For example, we know of a few temples that were located in sacred groves outside of Rome. Most famous was the sanctuary of Diana in the wood of Nemi. The temple was built beside a small lake inside the grove, about sixteen miles from Rome. Archaeologists have found numerous clay figurines at the site, left as offerings by grateful worshippers.

Another much-loved sacred site was the source of the Clitumnus River, a tributary of the Tiber. The author-senator Pliny the Younger has left us this description:

There is a fair-sized hill, dark with ancient cypress-woods. Beneath this the spring rises, gushing out in several veins of

The emperor Hadrian had this statue of a river god set up on the grounds of his villa, or country retreat.

unequal size. After the initial flow has smoothed out, it spreads into a broad pool, pure and clear as glass, so that you can count the coins that have been thrown into it. . . . Near it there is an ancient and venerable temple. In it stands [an image of] Clitumnus himself, clothed, and draped in a crimson-bordered robe. . . . Around this temple there are several smaller shrines, each with its god. Every one has its own cult [worship dedicated to it], its own name, and some even their own springs.

The Romans firmly believed that every place had a guardian spirit, its *genius loci,* "the spirit of the place." Sometimes, as with Clitumnus, the name of the *genius* was known; sometimes it was not. Either way, the Romans believed that these powers should be honored. Many soldiers stationed at outposts in the provinces seem to have been particularly careful to honor such spirits. Archaeologists have found a number of altars dedicated to the "*genius* of this place" at forts on the empire's frontiers. But with or without temples, altars, shrines, or statues, the presence of the divine in nature remained clear to many Romans. The philosopher-statesman Seneca eloquently expressed this feeling in a letter to one of his friends:

> If you have ever come on a dense wood of ancient trees that have risen to an exceptional height, shutting out all sight of the sky with one thick screen of branches upon another, the loftiness of the forest, the seclusion of the spot, your sense of wonderment at finding so deep and unbroken a gloom out of doors, will persuade you of the presence of a deity. Any cave in which the rocks have been eroded deep into the mountain resting on it, its hollowing out into a cavern of impressive extent not produced by the labours of men but the result of the processes of nature, will strike into your soul some inkling of the divine.

IV
RELIGIOUS ROLES FOR MEN

Each hour be minded, valiantly as becomes a Roman
and a man, to do what is to your hand, with . . .
unaffected dignity, natural love, freedom, and justice. . . .
You see how few things a man need master in order
to live a smooth and godfearing life.
—Marcus Aurelius, *Meditations*

he model of Roman manhood was Aeneas. In Virgil's *Aeneid,* the hero is frequently called *pius* Aeneas because of his supreme devotion to duty. A favorite subject in Roman art was Aeneas carrying his weak and aged father away from the conquered city of Troy. Aeneas's *pietas* toward his father was only surpassed by his *pietas* toward Jupiter, the father of the gods. At every turn, the hero followed the god's will, even when it caused him great personal unhappiness. Having fled the destruction of the Trojan War, he knew that his duty was to follow Jupiter's guidance and find a new home for himself and all who depended on him.

opposite: Aeneas carries his father away from war-torn Troy. The great seventeenth-century sculptor Bernini created this beautiful statue.

31

Aeneas's fatherly concern for his people mirrored the fatherliness of Jupiter. Fatherliness, in fact, was one of the most valued qualities in ancient Rome. It was expected especially from leaders, whether in the government, the army, the local community, or the family. And whether a man was *pater patriae,* the father of the country (ruler of the empire), or *pater familias,* the father of a family (head of the household), he had the responsibility of ensuring that everyone who depended on him would enjoy the peace of the gods.

A FATHER'S DUTIES

Home-based worship was a very important part of Roman religion. It was a father's duty to lead this worship, acting as a priest for his entire household, including slaves as well as family members. He was responsible for maintaining a *lararium,* the family shrine to the Lares. This could be a freestanding shrine, a wall niche, or even a painting on the wall. In well-to-do homes, it was generally located in the garden, kitchen, or atrium, which was something like a modern living room. Some men, including the emperor Augustus, also had a *lararium* in their bedroom. One of the first things a pater familias did after getting up in the morning was light incense at the *lararium,* and he might worship the Lares in this way again at bedtime.

At dinnertime, the family honored the Lares, Penates, and the goddess Vesta. Traditionally, the whole household gathered in front of the *lararium* to call on the deities before going to the table. After the appetizer course, the family was silent while the father made an offering by throwing *mola salsa* and a choice piece of meat into the hearth fire or a small altar fire. These ancient customs were cherished by many Romans. The poet Horace, for example,

This wall-niche *lararium* from Pompeii shows the father of the family with a Lar dancing on each side of him. The snake symbolizes the father's *genius*, or guardian spirit.

wrote, "O, divine nights and meals where we eat, my family and I, before the Lar of my own home."

The pater familias was also responsible for maintaining a proper relationship between his family and the dead. In the *lararium,* or in another special place, he kept busts or wax masks of his ancestors. During the festival of Lemuria (May 9, 11, and 13), he had to make sure that unhappy ghosts would not harm the living. Each of the three nights, when everyone else was asleep, the pater familias got up, made a gesture against evil, and washed his hands. Then, barefoot, he walked through the house with nine black beans, food for the dead because beans were believed to contain a kind of life force of their own. He threw them back over his shoulder one at a time, proclaiming, "With these beans I redeem both myself and my household." When his task was done, this

A LANDOWNER'S PIETAS

In North Africa around 156 c.e., Apuleius was accused of having used magic to get a wealthy widow to marry him. In his successful defense speech, he portrayed himself as a properly religious man. He pointed out that the prosecutor, on the other hand, was notable for his lack of *pietas* and neglected his duty to the spirits that inhabited the land he owned:

> Even to the rural deities who give him food and clothing he never once offers the first-fruits of his crops, his vines or his herds. On his lands there is not a single sanctuary or holy site or wood! And why mention groves or chapels? Those who have been at his place declare they have never seen so much as a stone anointed with oil or a branch adorned with a garland anywhere on his estate.

In contrast, here is a passage from the poet Martial (ca. 40–ca. 104), who has regretfully sold his farm and asks the buyer to honor the gods there as he has done:

> I entrust to your care these twin pine trees, the glory of their untilled grove, and these holm oaks, haunted by fauns [woodland spirits], and the altars of Jupiter, the thunder god, and shaggy Silvanus which my unlettered farm manager built with his own hands. . . . I also entrust to your care the virgin goddess [Diana] of the sacred sanctuary and Mars, who ushers in my year . . . , and also the laurel grove of tender Flora. . . . Whether you propitiate all the kindly deities of my tiny little farm with a blood sacrifice or incense, please tell them this: "Wherever your Martial is, though absent, he is yet in spirit a suppliant with me, making this sacrifice to you. Consider him to be present and grant to each of us whatever we may pray for."

pious father could feel some assurance that the dead were satisfied and would not carry off any of his family to join them in the underworld.

PRIESTS OF THE STATE

As it was a father's duty to maintain the *pax deorum* for his family, other men took this responsibility on behalf of the state as a whole. First and foremost in this role was the emperor himself. He was the *pontifex maximus,* the chief priest and head of the state religion. All other priests in the city were appointed by the emperor, and they held their positions for life. These men were wealthy, educated senators, whose religious duties were only part-time. About one-quarter to one-third of Roman senators served as priests. This mix of priesthood and politics may seem odd to us, but it made perfect sense to the Romans. As Cicero explained:

> Among the many things . . . that our ancestors created and established under divine inspiration, nothing is more renowned than their decision to entrust the worship of the gods and the highest interests of the state to the same men— so that the most eminent and illustrious citizens might ensure the maintenance of religion by the proper administration of the state, and the maintenance of the state by the prudent interpretation of religion.

The city of Rome had sixteen priests called pontiffs (in Latin, *pontifices*). They oversaw such matters as adoptions, wills, and burials. Traditionally, they were also in charge of the calendar (setting the dates of movable holidays, for example) and of recordkeeping

A priest preparing for the sacrifice of a pig. At sacrifices, Roman priests covered their heads so that they would be less likely to see or hear anything unlucky that might mar the ceremony.

for the city. Mainly, though, they were experts in religious law. They made sure that government officials who had religious duties performed them properly, and also oversaw "all the priesthoods" and their helpers "to make sure that they commit no error in regard to the sacred laws," as historian Dionysius of Helicarnassus wrote. He added, "For private citizens who are not knowledgeable about religious matters concerning the gods and divine spirits, the *pontifices* are explainers and interpreters." Rome's pontiffs could exercise authority in nearby towns and cities, but not in the provinces. Roman colonies had their own pontiffs as well as augurs.

Fifteen priests known as flamens also belonged to the college, or association, of pontiffs. Each flamen served one particular deity. Most important was the Flamen Dialis, the priest of Jupiter. Unlike the other flamens, he had to follow a number of ancient rules. For example, he could not touch a dead body, he could not be absent from Rome for longer than several days at a time, and he had to have been married only once and in the most formal type of wedding ceremony. His wife, the Flaminica Dialis, assisted him in some of his duties and had to follow the same rules. Other Italian towns, as well as Roman colonies, also had flamens. In addition, priests who looked after the worship of the deified emperors, both in Rome and the provinces, were called flamens.

The god Mars, who had his own priest, the Flamen Martialis

The augurs formed another major priestly college. They interpreted the will of the gods and laid out sacred space. The college had sixteen members, one of whom was the emperor. There were several other priesthoods in Rome. Among them was the twelve-member Arval Brotherhood, which performed regular sacrifices for the health of the emperor and his family. The Salii were twenty-four priests of Mars, famous for the leaping dances they performed at certain festivals in the god's honor.

Most priests of the state religion were not assigned to serve in any particular temple. Each temple, however, had its own custodian living next to it. If an individual wanted to make a sacrifice at the temple, the custodian was the one who would arrange it. In addition, he was in charge of looking after the building and had a staff of servants and slaves to do the actual work of keeping the temple clean and in good repair. Many temples also had gatekeepers, clerks, guides for visitors, and other workers.

FOR MEN ONLY

Many men were drawn to the mystery religions. Some were initiated into the Mysteries of Demeter and Persephone, others became priests of Cybele, and still others, like Apuleius, devoted themselves to Isis. But perhaps the most popular mystery religion for men was that of Mithras. In fact, only men were allowed to become initiates of Mithras. The god was particularly attractive to soldiers, who carried Mithraism (along with traditional Roman religion) throughout the empire.

A priest of the goddess Cybele, shown with cymbals and other objects used in her worship

Although Mithras was originally a Persian god, his worship in the Roman Empire took on its own unique form. Its ceremonies were secret, but literature and archaeology have revealed some information. Group worship took place in caves or small, cavelike rooms. A bull sacrifice played a major role, since Mithras had slain a great bull in order to give life to the earth. There were also rites of purification and ceremonial meals of bread and water, or perhaps wine mixed with water. Initiates of Mithras progressed through seven ranks, known as Raven, Bridegroom, Soldier, Lion, Persian, Sun Runner, and Father. Each of these was associated with a planet, and astrology seems to have played some role in Mithraism. But as with the other mystery religions (and even with some aspects of Rome's state religion), it is almost impossible for scholars today to know or understand many details of the worshippers' beliefs and practices.

This second-century statue from Rome's port city, Ostia, shows Mithras slaying the great bull.

WOMEN AND WORSHIP

hen we want to study women's experiences in the Roman world, we run into a very large problem: almost nothing written by any Roman woman has survived to the present.

In general, male authors were not interested in describing many aspects of women's lives, especially their thoughts and feelings. Men often looked down on women, and wrote about them mainly to criticize or make fun of them. Roman law actually placed most women in the same legal position as children. With few exceptions, women were required to have male guardians throughout their lives. In the area of religion, writers often painted women's beliefs and practices as being irrational and superstitious. Luckily, in recent years scholars have been

opposite:
Three women getting ready for a ceremony dedicated to Bacchus. The Mysteries of Bacchus gave women many opportunities for religious involvement.

making good progress in giving us a fairer and more realistic picture of Roman women.

THE VESTAL VIRGINS

As we have seen, political leadership and religious leadership were closely related. Although we know of a few examples of women in public office in cities in Roman-ruled Greece and Asia Minor, there were no government positions open to women in Rome itself. As a result, the roles they could play in the state religion were quite limited. For example, women were rarely, if ever, allowed to preside over blood sacrifices. However, Rome had one priesthood of women that was considered all-important to the well-being of the city and empire. The women of this priesthood were known as Vestal Virgins.

There were six Vestal Virgins. Chosen for their office between the ages of six and ten, they were from upper-class families and had to be physically perfect and to have both parents still living. They went to live at the House of Vesta in the Forum, where they would spend a total of thirty years: ten being trained, ten actively performing religious duties, and ten teaching the younger Vestals. During this time, they could not have any relationships with men. If they did, they were put on trial by the pontiffs and executed if found guilty. After their thirty years of service, they were free to return to their family homes and get married. Most, however, chose to remain in the House of Vesta. As Dionysius of Helicarnassus observed, "The Vestal Virgins receive many fine honors from the city and do not therefore yearn for children or marriage."

Vestals did enjoy privileges that most other Roman women did not. A vestal was freed from her father's authority and could make a will and give legal testimony without a guardian's oversight. Like a male officeholder, a Vestal had an attendant called a lictor walk before her when she went out. If she happened to come upon a criminal being led to execution, he was immediately pardoned because of the power of her sacred presence. Prime seats were even reserved for the Vestals in the theater. The state paid them a salary that covered all their living expenses and then some. The Vestal Virgins, in fact, made up Rome's only full-time, paid priesthood.

The goddess Vesta (*seated*) with four Vestal Virgins

These honors came to the Vestals because their duties were believed to guarantee the health and safety of the state. They participated in important processions and ceremonies. They made the *mola salsa* that was used in major sacrifices. They guarded the city's most ancient holy objects, said to have been brought from Troy by Aeneas himself. Most importantly, the Vestals tended the eternal flame of the sacred fire in the temple of Vesta. This was the hearth fire of all Romans, and as long as it continued to burn, Rome would stay strong.

PRIESTESSES AND WORSHIPPERS

Just as many emperors were deified after death, so were some empresses, and honor might be paid to an empress's *iuno* just as to an emperor's *genius*. Some women in the imperial family acted as priestesses in the worship of the deified emperors and empresses. It

Three priestesses taking part in a procession

appears that quite a few women in the eastern part of the empire, and even in some Italian towns, were priestesses responsible for honoring the imperial *genius* and *iuno*. For example, an inscription commemorates an Italian woman named Cassia Cornelia, "priestess of Augusta [a title of the empress] and our fatherland." Such women were leading citizens of their communities. They were also extremely wealthy—part of their priestly role involved paying for sacrifices, religious festivals, and public entertainments. Often these women's husbands also served in the imperial worship, but it seems that many or most of the priestesses held their titles and offices in their own right.

In Greece and Asia Minor, women could be priestesses of Greek gods or goddesses, especially of Artemis, goddess of women, mothers, the moon, and the wilderness. These same women often served in the imperial worship as well. The city of Perge in Asia Minor erected a statue to Plancia Magna, with an inscription on its base reading,

PRIESTESS OF ARTEMIS
AND BOTH FIRST AND SOLE PUBLIC PRIESTESS
OF THE MOTHER OF THE GODS
FOR THE DURATION OF HER LIFE
PIOUS AND PATRIOTIC

A second-century marble bust of a woman named Melitene, who was a priestess of the goddess Cybele

Plancia Magna gave her city a magnificent entrance gate that was decorated with statues and inscriptions honoring two deified emperors, a deified empress, and the reigning emperor and empress.

Women involved in the Mysteries of Demeter, Bacchus, Cybele, and Isis sometimes had the opportunity to become priestesses. Even those who did not take these leadership roles could still dedicate themselves to their beloved deity through initiation. Isis was especially attractive to women, who were given more respect and authority in the worship of this goddess than in any other sphere of Roman life. Isis was called the goddess of women, and at least one hymn to her proclaimed that she made women equal to men. She also embraced all social classes, including slaves and ex-slaves.

Isis was worshipped not only in private initiations but also in public ceremonies. For example, people gathered at her temple in Rome to sing

This woman, taking part in the Mysteries of Bacchus, may be dancing with a veil.

hymns every day as the doors were being opened in the morning and closed in the afternoon. And here is Apuleius's description of some of the women participating in a procession during a festival of Isis:

Women glowing in their white vestments moved with symbolic gestures of delight. Blossomy with the chaplets [wreathes] of the Spring, they scattered flowerets out of the aprons of their dresses. . . . Others, who bore polished mirrors on their backs, walked before [the statue of] the Goddess and reflected all the people coming-after as if they were advancing towards the Image. Others, again, carrying combs of ivory, went through the various caressive motions of combing and dressing the queenly tresses of their Lady; or they sprinkled the street with drops of unguent [perfumed oil]. . . . Then there came walking a great band of men and women of all classes and ages, who had been initiated into the Mysteries of the Goddess and who were all clad in linen garments of the purest white.

Women's religious activities were not limited to priesthoods or to the Mysteries. Although fathers played the main role in family worship, mothers did take part by tending the hearth, taking care of

⟿ SULPICIA AT JUNO'S TEMPLE ⟾

Sulpicia, a first-century poet, is the only Roman woman whose literary works have come down to us today. The following poem may have been written by one of the men who belonged to the same literary circle as Sulpicia, or it may be one that she wrote about herself. In either case, it gives us a marvelous picture of a young Roman woman celebrating her birthday with a visit to Juno's temple.

> Juno of birthdays, accept the heaps of holy frankincense
> That the learned girl gives to you with tender hand.
> Today all is for you; for you, she has most joyously arrayed herself
> That, worthy to be seen, she may stand before your altars.
> Certainly, Goddess, you are the reason she is all dressed up—
> There is, however, one other she secretly would like to please.
> But you, Holy One, be favorable, so that no one may tear lovers apart,
> And prepare the same bonds for the young man as for her.
> You'll do well to unite them this way: there's no more deserving girl
> For him to serve, no worthier man for her. . . .
> Grant your approval and come, in your radiant purple robe:
> Three times offering will be made to you with cake, Pure Goddess, three times
> With unmixed wine. And the eager mother advises her daughter what to pray for;
> The girl asks something else now, silently in her mind. . . .
> And may you also be gracious to the youth, so that when next year comes,
> This same longstanding love may still live in their prayers.

the *lararium,* and similar activities. Women could attend sacrifices and other public ceremonies of the state religion, even if their only role (as for most of the other people present) was to watch and keep silent. There were many goddesses whom women particularly favored and who were especially concerned with women's lives. On special occasions and in times of need, women commonly prayed and made offerings at the temples of these much-loved goddesses.

VI

THROUGH LIFE'S STAGES

THEY BELIEVED THAT THE GODS TOOK PART
IN ALL THEIR CONCERNS, AT ALL TIMES.
—PLINY THE ELDER, *NATURAL HISTORY*

The Romans felt that unseen powers were all around them. Some, like the great gods, were interested in humans and their cares. Others were impersonal spirits or natural forces. Since these could still affect humans, for good or ill, it was important to behave properly toward them. Things like illness, bad luck, and envy were also powerful forces, and these had to be guarded against. The awareness that gods and spirits of various kinds were always present and active determined many of the customs that accompanied the Romans through the stages of their lives.*

*The customs and traditions we know about are mainly those of the upper class. Very few people outside of this class had the opportunity to record their beliefs, thoughts, feelings, and experiences. In fact, most people in the Roman Empire did not know how to read or write.

BIRTH AND CHILDHOOD

This scene from a myth about the birth of Jupiter shows how a newborn Roman baby, wrapped in swaddling, was presented to the father for the first time.

In the ancient world, birth could be a dangerous and frightening experience. Medical knowledge was limited, so many mothers and babies died during or soon after birth. Infants born healthy might not stay that way for long: about 45 percent of Roman children did not reach their tenth birthday. Given this situation, parents often sought divine help to protect their children.

Women prayed to Diana, Juno Lucina, or a water goddess named Egeria to give them safe pregnancies, easy labors, and healthy babies. For several nights after the birth, three men of the household carried out a protective ceremony, striking the threshold with an axe, then with a pestle, then sweeping the threshold with a broom. The *numina* of these tools of civilization would defend the newborn from Silvanus and other wild spirits. For further divine protection, the family set up a bed for Juno and a table for Hercules in the atrium, as well as a table where the mother's friends could leave offerings for the gods.

Eight days after birth for a girl, and nine for a boy, the baby was purified and named. At this time, many Romans believed, goddesses of fate would decide the child's destiny. Family members were on the lookout for bolts of lightning or other signs from the gods that might give them a hint of what the baby's future held.

Every stage of a child's development was watched over or empowered by a particular deity or *numen*. There were, for exam-

❧ BIRTHDAY PORRIDGE ❧

Birthdays were important family occasions for Romans of all ages. The traditional food for these celebrations was pottage, or porridge. Pliny the Elder explained that the early Romans "lived for a long time not on bread but on pottage. . . . Consequently the oldest sacred rites and birthdays are celebrated with sacrificial pottage."

We might not know how to make sacrificial pottage today, but several other Roman pottage recipes have come down to us. Most combine unground, boiled spelt (a red-grained wheat) with olive oil, spices, and peas or lentils. Some versions add ground meat and a little wine to the mix. Here is an adaptation of a Roman cookbook's recipe for a slightly different, but easy to make, kind of pottage:

Pultes Tractogalatae (Bread and Milk Porridge)
Put a pint of milk and a little water into a saucepan and warm over low heat. Crumble three pieces of dry bread and add them to the milk. Gently stir from time to time. When the mixture is heated through, add honey to make the porridge as sweet as you want it. *Gusta!* (Taste and enjoy!)

ple, Edusa and Potina to teach it to eat and drink; Ossipago and Carna to strengthen its bones and muscles; Fabulinus and Locutius to help it speak, first in single words and then in sentences; Numeria to help it learn to count; and Camena to teach it to sing.

Along with appealing to the appropriate deities or *numina,* parents had their children wear a round pendant called a *bulla* as protection against the destructive force of envy. Children also dressed in purple-bordered togas, like those worn by priests, to mark them as holy. And of course, parents were careful to teach their children proper *pietas* so that they would be able to do their part to maintain the *pax deorum* when they grew up.

This young boy's hairstyle, longer over the right ear, shows that he probably belonged to a family that worshipped Isis.

BECOMING AN ADULT

At around sixteen, a boy had his coming-of-age. Roman families often chose to celebrate this occasion on March 17, the festival of Liber, a god concerned with the growth of both humans and crops. The boy put aside his childhood clothes and for the first time donned the white toga of manhood. He took off his *bulla* and left it in the *lararium* as an offering to the family's guardian spirits. Then he, his parents, and their friends went to the Forum, where he was formally enrolled as a citizen. At the Capitol they made sacrifices to Jupiter and the goddess Iuventas (Youth). The celebration was completed with a feast held at the entrance to the family home—presumably so that everyone passing by would know the boy had become a man. The young man and his family

A child's gold *bulla*, found in the ruins of Pompeii

celebrated again when he had his first shave, around the age of twenty-one. The shaved-off beard was offered to the Lares.

There was no coming-of-age ceremony for girls, who might marry as young as twelve. A wedding day had to be chosen carefully, because many days (including the entire month of May) were unlucky for beginning a marriage. The night before a girl's wedding, she gave her *bulla* to the Lares while her father made an offering of incense. At or before dawn the next day, her mother helped her dress in her bridal clothes, which included a straight white tunic and a red or orange-yellow veil. Her hair was arranged in a style said to symbolize modesty (it was the same hairstyle worn by the Vestals), and she also wore a wreath of herbs and flowers that were considered lucky.

The wedding ceremony took place at the bride's home. It began with an animal sacrifice and could not continue until a *haruspex*

A nineteenth-century artist painted this scene of a Roman bride, her new husband beside her, making an offering.

examined the internal organs and announced that the gods approved of the marriage. Then a married woman joined together the right hands of the bride and groom, and they stated their consent to be married. A procession accompanied by singers, flute players, and torchbearers led the bride to the groom's house. He carried her over the threshold so that she would not stumble, which would foretell bad luck for the marriage. Next the new wife ceremoniously offered her husband fire and water, symbols of the necessities of life and also of the elements that come together to create new life. After this he presented her to his Lares, and then the wedding feast could begin.

DEATH

People had different ideas about the reasons for life's difficulties. For some, it was a matter of fate. For others, what happened to them was simply due to random chance or luck. To the philosopher-emperor Marcus Aurelius, fate and luck operated together with the gods: "The work of the gods is full of Providence [Fate]: the work of Fortune is not divorced from nature or the spinning and winding of the threads ordained by Providence." Another popular opinion was that problems were the gods' way of testing and strengthening humans. To this idea, Seneca added, "It is not what you endure, but how you endure it that is important."

One way or another, though, death finally came to everyone. The spirit Caeculus took away the dead person's sight, and Viduus separated the soul from the body. Members of the household laid out the corpse, washed it, and perfumed it with cedar oil, honey, and myrrh. The body was then placed on a flower-decked bed in the atrium, where incense was constantly kept burning. Women

Musicians often accompanied funeral processions.

were hired to lament the deceased, often to the accompaniment of flute players. After a week, the funeral procession set out for the family tomb. Escorting the deceased were musicians, torchbearers, and men carrying the masks or busts of the ancestors. The children of the dead person marched along dressed all in black.

At or near the tomb, the body was laid on a funeral pyre and cremated. Then family members sprinkled the ashes with wine and milk, dried them, and put them into a marble urn in the tomb. After circling the tomb three times and calling out a last farewell to the deceased, they returned home. They sacrificed a ram to the Lares, then shared the traditional funeral meal of eggs, beans, lentils, and chicken. For nine more days of mourning, none of the family did any work. At the end of this period, wine and milk were offered to the spirits of the dead, and then the survivors could resume their normal lives.

People had varying ideas about what happened after death. The most common belief was that the spirits of the dead lived on in the underworld, which they could occasionally leave to interact with the living. These spirits were called the Manes (MAH-nays) or *divi parentes,* "divine ancestors." They were honored at major Roman festivals every year.

THROUGH LIFE'S STAGES

VII

ROMAN HOLIDAY

THIS IS A SACRED DAY. PLOUGHMAN AND EARTH MUST REST,
THE HEAVY PLOUGHSHARE HANG AT REST ON THE WALL.
UNHARNESS ALL THE YOKES: LET THE OXEN STAND AND FEAST
AT THE FULL MANGER, WEARING CROWNS OF FLOWERS.
EVERYTHING MUST KEEP HOLIDAY. . . .
—TIBULLUS, *ELEGIES*

here were many religious observances throughout the year. Some were full-blown festivals lasting an entire day or more, when no business was conducted and people gathered together for ceremonies and celebrations. Other occasions were half-day holidays. Most festivals occurred on the same date every year, but some were "movable feasts" (like modern Easter) whose exact date each year had to be set by the pontiffs. Unscheduled festivals could be declared, too—for example, to celebrate a military victory. Most official holidays fell on odd-numbered days, which were considered luckiest. State holidays were celebrated publicly with sacrifices and often with *ludi,* or games. These included chariot races, theatrical

opposite: Women, girls, and musicians on their way to the temple of Ceres to celebrate a springtime holiday. This painting is by Lawrence Alma-Tadema, a nineteenth-century artist who was famous for his well-researched portrayals of life in the ancient world.

✒ LET THE GAMES BEGIN! ☙

It can be difficult today to understand exactly how chariot races and similar events related to religion. Even for many Romans during the time of the emperors, the games were more important as a source of entertainment than as a religious observance. Nevertheless, honoring the gods with games was one of the traditional ways of reinforcing the *pax deorum*. The religious aspect of the games was made clear by the processions that began the events. Before a day of chariot racing, "floats" with statues of various deities entered the circus, or stadium, and went around the track. Ovid, famous for his long poems about mythology and love, described such a procession, including his personal thoughts during it. (He, or the character speaking in the selection, seems to have his mind on other things.)

Pay attention! It's time for applause. The golden procession has arrived. Victory is riding in front, her wings outstretched. Be with me, Victory, and make me victorious in love. You who trust yourselves to the sea can clap for Neptune. I have no interest in seafaring; I'm a landlubber. And you, there, soldier, clap for Mars, your patron god. I hate warfare. It's peace I like, and it's in peace that you find love. Let Phoebus [Apollo] help the augurs, and Phoebe [Diana] the hunters. Minerva, seek applause from the craftsmen. Farmers, stand up! Here comes Ceres and delicate Bacchus. Boxers should show reverence to Pollux and horsemen to Castor. Now it's my turn to applaud, sweet Venus, for you and your archer cupids. Nod in support of my plans, oh goddess. Make my new girlfriend receptive to my advances and willing to be loved.

productions, and other spectacles. Admission was free, and vast crowds attended.

The Romans also recognized private holidays, which were family occasions, such as birthdays. (The emperor's birthday, however, called for a grand public celebration.) All important family events were generally marked by prayers to the Lares and Penates. In addition, families gave special worship to these spirits on the first of each month (called the Kalends), roughly a week later (the Nones), and in the middle of the month (the Ides). On these days, the mother decorated the hearth with flower garlands, and the father burned incense and made other offerings to the family guardians. Typical offerings, especially on the Kalends, were honeycombs, grapes, and cakes. The poet Tibullus, away from home, fondly recalled these occasions: "If only I could once again celebrate the Penates of my ancestors, and each month pay homage of incense to the ancient Lar!"

MONTH BY MONTH

Many Roman holidays are difficult to understand today, even for scholars. People often wonder what a particular holiday was about, what its meaning was, or what worshippers were seeking through their actions. In a number of cases, by the time of the emperors the answers to these questions had been forgotten by the Romans themselves. For most Romans, it was enough to know that their ancestors had celebrated these same holidays, with the same ceremonies, for generation after generation. One of the best ways to maintain the *pax deorum* was to keep tradition alive.

All the same, at least some of the reasons for a number of the year's festivities seem clear. For example, the names of many of the months can tell us a lot about what deities were especially honored then and what types of ceremonies took place. The agricultural cycle was also extremely important, because even the most city-bred Romans were well aware that they depended on the earth's production of crops.

January was named after Janus, the god of beginnings, gates, and doorways. His festival, January 1, marked the start of the new year. People celebrated by giving one another small gifts and were careful to speak only of good things all day. On January 3, the Arval Brotherhood vowed sacrifices to the Capitoline Triad and other deities for the well-being of the emperor and his family during the coming year; they also carried out the sacrifices that they had vowed the previous January. Around the same time, Compitalia was celebrated so that people could honor the Lares of the crossroads. January 11 brought Carmentalia, dedicated to Carmentis, a goddess who presided over birth. Toward the end of the month came Sementivae, a country festival that prepared seeds for sowing, with prayers and sacrifices to Ceres and Mother Earth.

Februa meant "offerings or ceremonies for purification," and this was a theme in February's major festivals. February 15 was Lupercalia. Priests called Luperci (literally, "wolfmen") made a sacrifice at the place where Rome's founder, Romulus, and his brother, Remus, were said to have been nursed by a wolf after being abandoned in the wilderness. Following the sacrifice, the Luperci, clothed in goatskin, ran through the streets of Rome. Crowds turned out to watch them, and they struck everyone they met with goatskin

Ceres, with the wheat that was her special concern, by an eighteenth-century painter thongs. This was an act of purification, and people also believed that it would help women who were having trouble becoming pregnant.

Roman festivals sometimes overlapped one another, and Lupercalia came in the middle of Parentalia, February 13–21. The dead were said to wander freely during Parentalia. Temples were closed, but people set out offerings of food and flowers for the dead and held feasts at the tombs of their ancestors. Then, on the twenty-second, Caristia was devoted to renewing family ties, patching up quarrels, and honoring the Lares.

Mars was the namesake of March, when his priests performed their leaping dance on two different holidays and military trumpets were purified. April seems to have been Venus's month and was the favorite time for Roman weddings. In the countryside, agricultural activities were really getting under way, so April also saw a number of festivals related to the earth and farming—for example, the seven-day Cerialia, devoted to the grain goddess Ceres. April 21 was Parilia, in rural Italy a festival to honor the divine guardian of shepherds and their flocks. This was also the official date of Rome's founding, so in the city people celebrated Rome's birthday. Both the rural and urban festivities featured bonfires that people leaped over for good luck.

Flora, the goddess of flowers, painted by the great Renaissance artist Titian

Floralia, the feast of the flower goddess Flora, began on April 28 and lasted through May 3. May was named after Maia, a goddess of growing things. She was said by some to be the mother of Mercury, who shared a festival with Jupiter on May 15. Before this, however, came Lemuria, when fathers protected their households from troublesome ghosts. The end of the month brought Ambarvalia. For this festival of purification, people called on Ceres, Bacchus, Jupiter, Mars, and Janus. To drive away harmful forces, farmers led a sheep, a pig, and an ox around the boundary of their fields; in the city, the same three animals were led around the *pomerium*. The animals were then sacrificed, and the rest of the day was spent in feasting and merrymaking.

So the year went, each month with its festivals to honor the gods, the land, and the history of Rome. The year ended with the most joyous holiday of all, Saturnalia. It began on December 17 and continued through the twenty-third. On the first day, there was a sacrifice at the temple of Saturn with a public feast afterward. During the festival, people wore bright-colored clothes, went to parties, exchanged gifts and good wishes, and gave their slaves time off. The author Macrobius recorded that, in addition, "households faithful to the rites honour their slaves by serving them dishes first as if they were the masters." Everyone wore a soft felt cap like the one that was traditionally given to freed slaves, perhaps to show that during this time of year, at least, all human beings were equal. The festival was held in honor of the god Saturn, who was said to have been the first ruler of Italy, the one who gave people laws and taught them how to plant crops. As Virgil wrote, "His reign was the period called in legend the Golden Age, / So peacefully serene were the lives of his subjects."

WOMEN'S FESTIVALS

Some Roman holidays were mainly for women, or involved their active participation. This was especially true for matrons—freeborn married women—particularly those in the upper class. The holiday of Matronalia, on March 1, was dedicated to them and was rather

Women visit a temple of Venus in this scene imagined by a nineteenth-century painter.

like Mothers' Day. Women received gifts from their husbands and children; during the reign of Vespasian, the emperor himself gave presents to Rome's matrons. The women visited Juno's temple and offered flowers there.

The first of April was the Veneralia, and matrons went to the temple of Venus Verticordia, "Turner of Hearts," who strengthened marriages. Worshippers washed and dressed Venus's statue in the temple and drank a beverage made of milk, honey, and poppy seeds. Also on April 1, lower-class women honored Fortuna Virilis, the goddess of the Luck of Men, with ceremonies held in public bathhouses. The goddess of the Luck of Women—Fortuna Muliebris—doesn't seem to have had a particular holiday. But the empress Livia, Augustus's wife, was especially devoted to her and renovated her temple just outside of Rome.

The Vestalia arrived on June 9. On this occasion, Roman matrons took offerings to the temple of Vesta and were allowed into the holiest part of it, usually open only to the Vestal Virgins. The Matralia on June 11 was the day of Mater Matuta, Mother of the Dawn. Matrons celebrated it with their sisters and prayed for the well-being of one anothers' children. On August 13, there was a festival of Diana. Women wearing flower garlands went in a torch-lit procession to Diana's sanctuary in the grove of Nemi to thank her for answered prayers.

December 3 brought the festival of Bona Dea (the Good Goddess), which matrons and the Vestal Virgins celebrated in the home of a leading government official. All males, including children and slaves, had to leave before preparations could even begin. Then the official's wife or mother decorated the house with vines and other greenery. Priestesses of Bona Dea, who were ex-slaves, brought the statue of the goddess from her temple for the occasion and probably also took part in the ceremonies. These were held at night, and the celebration included a feast, music, singing, and dancing. Many people believed that if these festivities were disturbed or interrupted, the well-being of all Romans would be endangered.

~VIII~
CONFLICT AND TOLERANCE

THROUGHOUT THE WHOLE FAR-FLUNG EMPIRE, . . .
WE SEE THAT EACH LOCAL GROUP OF PEOPLE
HAS ITS OWN RELIGIOUS RITUALS AND WORSHIPS LOCAL GODS. . . .
THE ROMANS, HOWEVER, WORSHIP ALL THE GODS IN THE WORLD.
—MINUCIUS FELIX, *OCTAVIUS*

ome's religion developed over centuries, and was continuously evolving. With their value for tradition, the Romans rarely dropped time-honored religious practices, but they generally had no problem adding on new gods, new holidays, and new ceremonies or prayers. When Rome conquered a territory, often the deities of that place were formally invited to join the Roman gods. And generally, the residents of conquered lands were permitted to continue their own traditional worship. Emperors even instructed provincial governors to preserve the local holy places.

Under Roman influence, however, the native deities of many provinces underwent a transformation, becoming more Roman

This statue from Gaul, made not long after the region was conquered by Rome, probably depicts a mother goddess and her divine child.

themselves. This happened most obviously in Gaul (modern France and Belgium) and Britain. Before conquest, people in these provinces seldom carved stone images of their deities. After conquest, sculptures of British and Gaulish deities became quite common. The gods and goddesses were frequently portrayed wearing Roman clothing and hairstyles. Often they received Roman names as well, added to their original name and based on the Roman deity to whom they seemed most similar. So, for example, the British goddess Sul became Sul Minerva. A great many British and Gaulish gods were identified with Mars, Mercury, Jupiter, and Apollo, resulting in "combination gods" such as Mars Camulos, Mercury Artaios, Jupiter Taranis, and Apollo Belenus.

One thing that Roman authorities could not accept either in the provinces or at home was a threat to order. There was a difference between religion, which followed proper forms, and superstition. To the Romans, superstition was irrational, overly emotional devotion that resulted in worshippers thinking more of themselves and the otherworld than of the community and this world. This posed one kind of threat. Another came from religious groups, such as the Mysteries, that had their own organization independent of the state. Emperors often feared that any group—religious or otherwise—with its own leaders and treasury might oppose government authority or even start a rebellion. A few religious communities, it seems, did in fact agitate to overthrow Roman rule in some provinces. For all these reasons, emperors from time to time tried to suppress (often violently) or regulate various religious groups, including Isis worshippers, the Druid priesthood of Gaul and Britain, and Christians.

RELIGION AND PATRIOTISM

When Jesus of Nazareth said, "Render to Caesar* the things that are Caesar's, and to God the things that are God's," he was expressing a separation of government and religion that was totally new. For the ancient Romans, it was perfectly natural for religion and politics to mix. As we have seen, they firmly believed that proper worship of the gods was necessary for the well-being of the city and the entire empire. Participating in the public ceremonies of the state religion was an act of patriotism. Refusing to take part in these rites could be seen as an act of treason. This attitude was problematic for Jews and Christians, who acknowledged only one god and often felt that participating in Roman ceremonies was a betrayal of their beliefs.

The Roman authorities tended to be more tolerant of Jews than of Christians. Even though Jewish beliefs and practices were very different from Roman ones, Judaism was understandable as the traditional religion of a particular people. Nevertheless, there were individuals in the Roman Empire who were terribly prejudiced, even to the point of violence, against Jews. And when the Jewish province of Judaea rebelled against Roman rule in 66–73 C.E., the empire was merciless. Roman troops destroyed the Temple in Jerusalem, the Jews' most sacred place, forever changing the nature of Jewish religious practice.

Roman soldiers in a triumphal procession carry a menorah and other objects looted from the Temple in Jerusalem.

*Caesar was used as a title for all Roman emperors.

~ THE EMPEROR AND THE ~ JEWISH COMMUNITY

Jews lived throughout the Roman Empire, but many of their beliefs and customs—especially their belief in one god—set them apart from their neighbors. Jews generally did not try to win converts and simply wished to be allowed to practice their religion in peace. Unfortunately, there were always people who were suspicious of them because of their different customs. Emperors varied in their attitudes toward the Jewish community. The Jewish philosopher Philo, in a letter to the third emperor, Gaius Caligula, reminded him of the first emperor's tolerance:

Augustus knew that a large part of Rome . . . was occupied and inhabited by Jews. . . . They were not forced to violate their ancestral traditions. Augustus knew that they have places for prayer meetings and that they meet together in these places, especially on the holy sabbaths when they come together as a group to learn their ancestral philosophy. He also knew that they take a first-fruit collection to raise money for religious purposes, and that they send this money to Jerusalem with people who will offer sacrifices. However, he did not banish them from Rome or deprive them of their Roman citizenship just because they were careful to maintain their identities as Jews. He did not force them to abandon their places for prayer meetings, or forbid them to gather to receive instruction in the laws, or oppose their first-fruit collections.

Augustus's successor, Tiberius, was less tolerant. He banished Jews, worshippers of Isis, and astrologers from the city of Rome. Although Gaius Caligula did reestablish the worship of Isis, he did not grant Jews the respect and tolerance requested by Philo. The fourth emperor, Claudius, expelled Christians from Rome (for "causing disturbances," according to the historian Suetonius), but seems to have been more generous toward Jewish communities outside the capital. Following is part of a letter he wrote to the people of Alexandria, Egypt, after a wave of violent conflicts between the Greek and Jewish populations in that city:

> . . . once again I conjure [urge] you that on the one hand the Alexandrians show themselves forbearing and kindly towards the Jews, who for many years have dwelt in the same city, and dishonor none of the rites observed by them in the worship of their god, but allow then to observe their customs as in the time of the deified Augustus, which customs I also, after hearing both sides, have sanctioned; and on the other hand I explicitly order the Jews not to agitate for more privileges than they formerly possessed. . . . If . . . you consent to live with mutual forbearance and kindliness, I on my side will exercise a solicitude of very long standing for the city, as one which is bound to us by traditional friendship.

Christianity was a new religion, without the respectability of a long history. Moreover, Christians actively worked to convince people to join them. This sort of thing had been almost unknown in the Greco-Roman world, and many people were highly offended by Christian efforts to make converts. Some Christians were very vocal about their contempt for traditional Roman religion, and some made a public point of refusing to honor the gods and the emperor's *genius*. To make matters worse, there were a few Christians who preached that the empire was evil and had to be destroyed so that the kingdom of God could be established on earth. When Roman authorities encountered such ideas, they decided that Christians were dangerous rebels.

Christians were first persecuted during the reign of the emperor Nero (54–68 C.E.), when he accused them of starting a fire that destroyed more than half of the city of Rome.

The historian Tacitus described what happened next:

> . . . people who admitted their belief were arrested, and then later, through their information, a huge crowd was convicted not so much of the crime of setting the fire, as of hating humankind. Mockery was heaped upon them as they were killed. . . . Nero offered his garden for this spectacle and provided circus entertainment where he put on a chariot driver's outfit and mingled with the crowd or stood in a chariot. And so pity arose, even for those who were guilty . . . since they seemed to have been slaughtered not for public good but to satisfy the cruelty of one man.

Fortunately, such persecutions were relatively rare, at least in the first two centuries C.E. Christians made up a very small percentage of the empire's population, and Roman authorities were generally content to leave them alone so long as they didn't cause any trouble.

THE IMMORTAL GODS

Most Romans felt that Jews and Christians were extremely intolerant to insist on the existence and worship of only one god. Traditional Roman religion, along with the Mysteries, remained strong throughout the 300s. By the 320s, however, the emperor Constantine was favoring Christianity over other religions. All but one of the emperors who came after him were Christians. Still, the vast majority of the empire's residents remained true to their ancient beliefs and practices. Emperors resorted to various techniques, including violence and persecution, to make their subjects convert to Christianity. In 391, Emperor Theodosius I

The Roman gods have lived on in artwork through the centuries. This statue of Bacchus is by Michelangelo.

outlawed all worship of the Roman deities and closed their temples. Yet even after this, devotion to the gods lived on, widespread and fairly open, for at least another century. Other changes came, especially following the fall of Rome in 476. Over the centuries, Christianity became more and more firmly entwined with the culture of Europe and, eventually, the Americas. But the names of our months have not changed since Roman times. People have continued to read the stories of Rome's deities in ancient works such as Virgil's *Aeneid* and Ovid's *Metamorphoses*. Images of the goddesses and gods continue to live, too, in countless beautiful paintings and sculptures. Even for people who no longer believe in these deities, there is still much to admire and much that can inspire.

Most inspiring of all, perhaps, is the vision of a world where people of many backgrounds and faiths can look past their differences, see their common humanity, and live together in harmony. This was the vision of Quintus Aurelius Symmachus. In 384 C.E., he pleaded with the emperor Valentinian II not to persecute the ancient Roman religion: "We are asking for amnesty for the gods of our fathers, the gods of our homeland." His eloquent defense of religious tolerance continued, in words that echo through the centuries:

This Roman copy of a Greek statue remains one of the most famous and well-loved images of the goddess Diana.

It is reasonable to assume that whatever each of us worships can be considered one and the same. We look up at the same stars, the same sky is above us all, the same universe encompasses us. What difference does it make which system each of us uses to find the truth? It is not by just one route that man can arrive at so great a mystery.

GLOSSARY

atrium the front room of a Roman house, used to receive visitors

augur a Roman priest with the responsibilities of marking out sacred space and of interpreting the will of the gods

auspices signs from the gods, particularly the behavior of birds within an area defined by the augurs

consecrate to make holy; to dedicate to religious purposes

equites members of Rome's second-highest class, ranking below senators. In general, they were wealthy businessmen. *Equites* literally means "horsemen" or "knights," because in early Roman times these were the men wealthy enough to afford warhorses and equipment for fighting on horseback.

forum the civic center and main meeting place of a Roman city, with government buildings, offices, shops, and temples surrounding a large open area. In Rome itself, there were six forums: the ancient original Forum, plus additional forums built by Julius Caesar and by the emperors Augustus, Nerva, Vespasian, and Trajan.

inscription words written on or carved into lasting materials such as metal and stone

Latin the Romans' language, and the official language of the empire. Greek was also widely used, especially in the eastern part of the empire.

matron a freeborn married woman

mola salsa grain that was roasted, ground, and mixed with salt, used to bless sacrificial animals and as an offering on its own

orator a person skilled in making speeches

personification a deity or imaginary being that represents a thing or idea

pontiff a member of a Roman priesthood concerned mainly with religious law. The Latin word is *pontifex,* and the plural form is *pontifices* (pohn-TI-fi-kays).

propitiate to seek the goodwill of the gods

province a territory of the Roman Empire

relief a form of sculpture in which the images project out from a flat surface

rotunda a very large, round room, typically with a domed roof

shrine a small place of worship, usually either outdoors or set aside inside a larger building (such as a wall niche holding a statue of a deity)

FOR FURTHER READING

Amery, Heather, and Patricia Vanags. *Rome & Romans.* London: Usborne, 1997.

Biesty, Stephen. *Rome in Spectacular Cross-Section.* New York: Scholastic Nonfiction, 2003.

Corbishley, Mike. *What Do We Know about the Romans?* New York: Peter Bedrick Books, 1991.

Ganeri, Anita. *How Would You Survive as an Ancient Roman?* New York: Franklin Watts, 1995.

Hart, Avery, and Sandra Gallagher. *Ancient Rome! Exploring the Culture, People and Ideas of This Powerful Empire.* Charlotte, VT: Williamson Publishing, 2002.

Hinds, Kathryn. *The Ancient Romans.* New York: Benchmark Books, 1997.

Hodge, Susie. *Ancient Roman Art.* Chicago: Heinemann Library, 1998.

Macdonald, Fiona. *Women in Ancient Rome.* New York: Peter Bedrick Books, 2000.

Nardo, Don. *Life in Ancient Rome.* San Diego: Lucent Books, 1997.

———. *The Roman Empire.* San Diego: Lucent Books, 1994.

ONLINE INFORMATION*

Carr, Karen E. *History for Kids: Ancient Rome.*
http://www.historyforkids.org/learn/romans/index.htm

Curran, Leo C. *Maecenas: Images of Ancient Greece and Rome.*
http://wings.buffalo.edu/AandL/Maecenas/general_contents.html

Goldberg, Dr. Neil. *The Rome Project.*
http://www.dalton.org/groups/rome/index.html

Illustrated History of the Roman Empire.
http://www.roman-empire.net

RELIGION

Michael C. Carlos Museum of Emory University. *Odyssey Online: Rome.*
   http://carlos.emory.edu/ODYSSEY/ROME/homepg.html

Pollard, Nigel. *Roman Religion Gallery.*
   http://www.bbc.co.uk/history/ancient/romans/roman_ religion_
   gallery.shtml

*All Internet sites were available and accurate when this book was sent to press.

BIBLIOGRAPHY

Adkins, Lesley, and Roy A. Adkins. *Dictionary of Roman Religion.* New
   York: Facts on File, 1996.

———. *Handbook to Life in Ancient Rome.* New York: Oxford University
   Press, 1994.

Apuleius. *The Golden Ass.* Translated by Jack Lindsay. Bloomington: Indiana
   University Press, 1962.

Beard, Mary, et al. *Religions of Rome. Volume I: A History.* Cambridge:
   Cambridge University Press, 1998.

Edwards, John. *Roman Cookery: Elegant & Easy Recipes from History's First
   Gourmet.* Rev. ed. Point Roberts, WA: Hartley & Marks, 1986.

Fantham, Elaine, et al. *Women in the Classical World: Image and Text.* New
   York: Oxford University Press, 1994.

Hallett, Judith P. "Women in the Ancient Roman World." In *Women's
   Roles in Ancient Civilizations: A Reference Guide,* edited by Bella
   Vivante, 257–289. Westport, CT: Greenwood Press, 1999.

Highet, Gilbert. *Poets in a Landscape.* New York: Alfred A. Knopf, 1957.

Kraemer, Ross Shepard. *Her Share of the Blessings: Women's Religions among
   Pagans, Jews, and Christians in the Greco-Roman World.* New York:
   Oxford University Press, 1992.

Lewis, C. Day, trans. *The Aeneid of Virgil.* Garden City, NY: Doubleday, 1953.

Lewis, Naphtali, and Meyer Reinhold, eds. *Roman Civilization, Sourcebook II: The Empire.* New York: Harper & Row, 1966.

MacMullen, Ramsay, and Eugene N. Lane. *Paganism and Christianity 100–425 C.E.: A Sourcebook.* Minneapolis: Fortress Press, 1992.

Meyer, Marvin W., ed. *The Ancient Mysteries: A Sourcebook.* San Francisco: Harper & Row, 1987.

Shelton, Jo-Ann. *As the Romans Did: A Sourcebook in Roman Social History.* 2nd ed. New York: Oxford University Press, 1998.

Turcan, Robert. *The Gods of Ancient Rome: Religion in Everyday Life from Archaic to Imperial Times.* Translated by Antonia Nevill. New York: Routledge, 2000.

Vitruvius. *The Ten Books on Architecture.* Translated by Morris Hicky Morgan. New York: Dover Publications, 1960.

Wells, Colin. *The Roman Empire.* 2nd ed. Cambridge, MA: Harvard University Press, 1992.

SOURCES FOR QUOTATIONS

Chapter I

p. 1 "Rome is a place": Turcan, *The Gods of Ancient Rome,* p. 148.

p. 1 "If we compare": ibid., p. 12.

p. 3 *redire ad Larem suum:* ibid., p. 16.

p. 7 "Alas, I suppose": author's translation of *Vae puto deus fio,* Suetonius, *Divus Vespasianus,* quoted in Adkins, *Dictionary of Roman Religion,* p. 106.

p. 8 "a feeling": MacMullen, *Paganism and Christianity,* p. 81.

p. 9 "Most holy and everlasting": Apuleius, *The Golden Ass,* pp. 250–251.

Chapter II

p. 11 "And what reason": MacMullen, *Paganism and Christianity,* p. 82.

p. 13 "It's not the abundance": online at *Ancient History Sourcebook,*
http://www.fordham.edu/halsall/ancient/personalrelig.html

p. 13 "It apparently does no good": Shelton, *As the Romans Did,* pp. 371–372.

p. 14 "Whether you are a god": author's adaptation of a prayer recorded
by Cato the Elder in *On Agriculture,* ibid., p. 363.

p. 14 "A memorandum to the god": ibid., p. 14.

p. 15 "There is indeed nobody": MacMullen, *Paganism and Christianity,*
pp. 22–23.

p. 19 "I approached the confines": Apuleius, *The Golden Ass,* p. 249.

Chapter III

p. 21 "We have a city": Beard, *Religions of Rome,* p. 168.

p. 22 "god-haunted feel": Lewis, *The Aeneid of Virgil,* p. 189.

p. 22 "In this grove": author's translation of *Aeneid,* Book VIII, lines 351–354.
Original Latin text at
http://www.thelatinlibrary.com/vergil/aen8.shtml

p. 23 "This will enable": Vitruvius, *The Ten Books on Architecture,* p. 116.

p. 24 "On June 21": Lewis, *Roman Civilization,* pp. 553–554.

p. 27 "There is a fair-sized": Highet, *Poets in a Landscape,* pp. 89–90.

p. 29 "If you have ever": MacMullen, *Paganism and Christianity,* p. 79.

Chapter IV

p. 31 "Each hour be minded": MacMullen, *Paganism and Christianity,* p. 107.

p. 33 "O, divine nights": Turcan, *The Gods of Ancient Rome,* p. 17.

p. 33 "With these beans": author's translation of Ovid, *Fasti,* Book V, line 438.

Original Latin text at
http://www.thelatinlibrary.com/ovid/ovid.fasti5.shtml

p. 34 "Even to the rural": Turcan, *The Gods of Ancient Rome,* p. 38.

p. 34 "I entrust to your care": Shelton, *As the Romans Did,* p. 369.

p. 35 "Among the many things": Beard, *Religions of Rome,* p. 115.

p. 36 "All the priesthoods": Shelton, *As the Romans Did,* p. 384.

p. 36 "to make sure" and "For private citizens": ibid., p. 385.

Chapter V

p. 41 "Women [are] the chief": Kraemer, *Her Share of the Blessings,* p. 3.

p. 42 "The Vestal Virgins": Shelton, *As the Romans Did,* p. 386.

p. 44 "priestess of Augusta": Fantham, *Women in the Classical World,* p. 362.

p. 45 "Priestess of Artemis": ibid., p. 363.

p. 46 "Women glowing": Apuleius, *The Golden Ass,* pp. 240–241.

p. 47 "Juno of birthdays": author's translation of Tibullus, *Elegies* III, xii.
© 2004 by Kathryn Hinds. Original Latin text at
http://www.thelatinlibrary.com/tibullus3.html

Chapter VI

p. 49 "They believed": author's translation from *Natural History,* Book 28. Original Latin text at
http://www.ukans.edu/history/index/europe/ancient_rome/L/
Roman/Texts/Pliny_the_Elder/28*.html

p. 51 "lived for a long time": Edwards, *Roman Cookery,* p. 66.

p. 51 recipe adapted from Edwards, p. 66.

p. 54 "The work of the gods": MacMullen, *Paganism and Christianity,* p. 107.

p. 54 "It is not what": Shelton, *As the Romans Did,* p. 430.

RELIGION

Chapter VII

p. 57 "This is a sacred day": Highet, *Poets in a Landscape,* p. 166.

p. 58 "Pay attention!": Shelton, *As the Romans Did,* pp. 340–341.

p. 59 "If only I could": Turcan, *The Gods of Ancient Rome,* p. 29.

p. 62 "households faithful": Turcan, *The Gods of Ancient Rome,* p. 35.

p. 62 "His reign was": Lewis, *The Aeneid of Virgil,* p. 189.

Chapter VIII

p. 65 "Throughout the whole": Shelton, *As the Romans Did,* p. 417.

p. 67 "Render to Caesar": *The Holy Bible,* Revised Standard Version,
      Mark 12:17.

p. 68 "Augustus knew": Shelton, *As the Romans Did,* p. 405.

p. 69 "causing disturbances": ibid., p. 408.

p. 69 "once again I conjure": MacMullen, *Paganism and Christianity,*
      pp. 155–156.

p. 70 "people who admitted": Shelton, *As the Romans Did,* p. 409.

p. 72 "We are asking": ibid., p. 391.

INDEX

ABOUT THE AUTHOR

KATHRYN HINDS grew up near Rochester, New York. In college she studied music and writing, and went on to do graduate work in comparative litera-ture and medieval studies at the City University of New York. She has written a number of books for young people, including Benchmark Books' LIFE IN THE MIDDLE AGES series and LIFE IN THE RENAISSANCE series. Kathryn now lives in Geor-gia's Blue Ridge Mountains with her husband, their son, two dogs, and three cats. When she is not writing, she enjoys danc-ing, reading, playing music, gardening, and taking walks in the woods.